Losing My Sunshine

A mother's grief in poetry and prose

SK Mustafa

FOR KADER

My only sunshine, my one true muse.

My Thanks to...

Hüseyin Hodja for inspiring me to start writing.

Özlem for convincing me to share my poetry.

Charlotte, Zed, Sana & Pat for your tireless encouragement and reassurance.

Neils for your selfless help with editing and e-book programming.

Günay (my sister) for your care and attentive eyes.

Naz for believing in me.

Chris for inspiring me.

Jeff for calming my soul with your music.

Mike for your time and support.

My parents for your love and loyalty.

The poetry community on Instagram for helping me to grow as a poet.

Kader for being my muse, my one true love, my EVERYTHING.

I love and appreciate you all so very much.

A Note from the Author

As this is a book about the loss of my child and my grief, please be aware that some of the contents will be sad, emotional and, in places, quite dark. There will of course be mention of death. Please read with care.

I am not someone who follows a religion as such, but I do have my faith. I mention God and Heaven and angels throughout this book but these are my own thoughts and beliefs – ones that sit well in my mind and heart and not ones of scripture. I have nothing to preach nor convince you of, as anything that I believe belongs to me alone. I respect whatever others believe or do not believe.

Thank you for reading.

Prologue

In 2007, I gave birth to a beautiful baby girl, Kader.

As a result of stress during labour, she suffered severe injury to her brain. The doctors did not envisage her being able to breathe on her own but after eleven days she started to do just that.

With many disabilities and illnesses, she was with me for six years and five months, until one winter's night when it came her time to leave.

Although she was unable to communicate with me, the bond we had was one that I could never have imagined. She was my absolute everything, my only sunshine.

This is for her. Everything is for her.

CONTENTS

Section Four: Milestones

Section Five: Grief's Battle

Section One:

The Beginning and the End

'She was here...
too beautiful to remain.'

-SK Mustafa

The Story

The story begins on a daunting afternoon
War breaks out in an expectant mother's womb
A little girl born broken and damaged
Breathing without support she cannot manage.

Connected to a machine for eleven days
As her fearful mother walks around in a haze
Doctors talking of a struggled existence
Advising switches be flicked, with persistence.

A father leaving the mother to decide
Behind fate and destiny the mother hides
Then baby starts to breathe on her own
And one month later, they take her home.

Soon thereafter three become two
When the father abandons them for God knows who
Struggle added onto existing struggle
Mother and baby continue in a dark but loving bubble.

For six years the two become inseparable
Never parting, even during stays in hospital
Until the night of that cold winter's day
When baby girl's time comes to pass away.

The story ends with a mother's eternal pain
After bidding farewell to her girl, too beautiful to remain
And while there's now a void in the arms of this mother
The long-absent father holds his child from another.

11th August 2007 (Part 1)

A first time mother
Ignored.
'Something is wrong'
Ignored.
'It doesn't feel right'
Ignored.

'This is labour!'
Mocked.
'You're not coping!'
Disgraced.
Leaving the room
Neglected.

Meconium stained
Heavy.
Baby left waiting
Suffocating.
Emergency declared
Too late.

Baby born quiet
Not breathing.
Baby resuscitated
Fitting.

Sedated and cleaned
Incubated.

Mother's anxiety
Blamed.
"Mother uncooperative"
Noted.
Mother bereaved
Life sentence.

~ ~ ~

As the Angels Played

And as the Angels played
One fell into my arms
Breaking her wing along the fall.

Taking her into my home, I tried to help
My human strength too weak to fix an Angel
I held her hand and loved her
                    and loved her
                      and loved her
Until the day He called her back home.

She is free now
Her wing has healed.

~ ~ ~

11th August 2007 (Part 2)

The silence, that's what I remember the most
The silence was so thick, like the heaviest of fogs
It was almost tangible
Dark, looming
Cold.
Silence.

The lack of a baby crying as she was cut out from her mother's womb
The lack of congratulations for the birth of a baby girl
The lack of answers to a mother questioning why her baby was not crying.
Silence.

Oh, how I remember that silence.
I will always remember that silence.

~ ~ ~

Silent Birth [an English sonnet]

You were my gift from up above that day
Though troubles loomed too close to hide from view
A gift that hurt herself along the way
A silent birth of which you made it through.

You chose to prove them wrong for what they said
They pressed that you were far from living on
That you would be too weak to leave your bed
But you would find your way, where you belong.

And though your time with me was short and toiled
You'd always find a way to smile and shine
Such memories will help to fill this void
But still, for you I'll always yearn and pine.

We were as one for all your time on earth
My gift that made it through her silent birth.

~ ~ ~

11th August 2007 (Part 3)

A glimpse of you in the cot is all they showed me
Before they rolled you off to Special Care
As I lay there getting stitched up.

> *I didn't get to see your beautiful face*
> *I didn't get to say hello or welcome you into the world*
> *I didn't get to give you my loving embrace.*

Another glimpse on *his* phone later that day
He took a photo when he popped in to visit you
As I lay in a separate room.
He'd later lose that photo
He wouldn't think to save it when he changed his phone.

One more little glimpse in the early hours of the next
morning before the transfer.

> *Still, no hello*
> *Still, no welcome*
> *Still, no embrace.*

I'm sorry, baby girl
Maybe all you needed was your mother's love.

~ ~ ~

Day 11

Breathing!
You're breathing!

My little ball of strength
So fragile, yet resilient
Swollen and bruised, yet thriving
Oh, how proud I am!

Breathing!
You're breathing!

Finally, I can hold you
Welcome you into the world
Smell you, kiss you
Love you!

Breathing!
You're breathing!

Please, baby girl...
Keep breathing!

~ ~ ~

28th *January 2014: Devastation*

Devastation
Forced its way into my veins
That lifeless day
And has since never gone away
Its poison merges
With blood and oxygen
Flowing through me
Every second, every day.

Screams
Forever forging in my mind
Blasting bloodied shockwaves through my brain
In my ears, ringing sirens of pain
Tears infused with vivid memories
Burning through my eyes
Momentarily blinded vision...

All I want to see is what I'll never see again.

~ ~ ~

Funeral

A big crowd
Sunshine
And earth.

A big crowd – so many here to tell you 'goodbye'
Some you knew, some you didn't
All touched by you in one way or another
I am overwhelmed. I am so proud!

Sunshine – it is cold but the day is bright
The sun is out and pouring its beauty onto your place of
rest
A gush of wind as you are placed lets me know you are
there
Thank you, sweet child, for being mine.

Earth – where your body will lay, as your soul drifts away.

Sleep well, dear one
Rest in eternal peace.
Till we meet again.

~ ~ ~

'Goodbyes are only for those who love with their eyes because for those who love with heart and soul there is no such thing as separation.'

-Rumi

Section Two:
Kader (My Angel Girl)

'...and I'll never comprehend how time didn't end when you did.'

-SK Mustafa

Kader

· /kahd.airr (roll the r!)

Days after you were born
I remember someone saying to me
'Give her a name'.
Your name had been put on a back burner
While I waited, helplessly, to see if you would survive.

I had picked a name for you, months before
One that I loved
From a song I would listen to on repeat as a child.
It no longer seemed to fit.

It dawned on me that the Turkish word for 'destiny'
Would be perfect for you
And I decided that day, you and I
Would live our destinies together
Whatever they would bring, we would face together
With love, with strength.
And so we did.

'Kader'... a name I don't hear much anymore from the mouths of others
'Kader'... a name I speak often
How that name suited you!
As you lived your destiny, with me

With a gleaming smile on your face
Like a soldier.
My little soldier!

My destiny, my strength, my life...
You were, and still are, all of these things.
What a team we made!
What a bond we had!

'Kader'...
Forever mine
And I, forever yours.

~ ~ ~

My Angel with Her Broken Wing

No future lay ahead of me, always binded to the past
It was plain to see, as clear as day I was going nowhere, fast.
For no reason that could be seen I was lost, there was something missing
Until the day He sent to me my Angel with her broken wing.

Though you brought with you such struggle, alongside so much pain
The strength of you, your courage and beauty, gave my world so much to gain.
I found myself much braver, you were my life, my only purpose
The confidence you gave to me allowed my strength to surface.
I gave to you my love and care but others could not see
That I needed you to give me guidance more than you needed me.

Our time as one was short yet sweet
Though nowhere near enough
And now I'm here without you, child
What could be than this more tough?

My dear sweet girl, my Destiny, I promise you with love
I will try to find my way to you, in heaven up above.
Until that day I bid to you, with pain, a sweet farewell
Sweet dreams to you my one true love, rest in peace my dear, sleep well.

~ ~ ~

*This is this first poem I wrote (22 February 2014).
I was inspired by a Hodja who, after performing her third night
prayers, read a poem he had written about me and Kader.
It was to become the beginning of my poetry journey.*

Sweet Angel Child of Mine (Betelgeuse)

One illuminating golden star
Among the silver
And underneath and to the right
Three linear stars shine bright
That's how I find you every night.

I wave and blow a heartfelt kiss
To you, a little girl I dearly miss.

You were mine.
Incomparably divine.

Sweet Angel Child of Mine.

~ ~ ~

*On one of the nights soon after laying Kader to rest, I was sitting out
in the garden looking up at the night sky. One bright star shone out at
me more than the rest and I felt like Kader was saying hello. That star
is Betelgeuse. To this day, I speak to it as if it is Kader.*

My Darling Angel Girl

Oh, how I miss you!
My darling Angel girl.

I feel my arms weaken day by every day
For not being able to wrap around you
I ache for not being able to see you, smell you, kiss you
Oh, how I miss you!
My one and only
My only Sunshine
Though your days here were grey
Your *smile* would brighten up the darkest of days
My darling Angel girl.

I feel such shame every time I scream your name
In anguish, in pain
I feel ridden by guilt
For my selfish yearning to have you by my side.
You are where you need to be
Where you belong
Where you are whole
Where you are free
My darling Angel girl.

Forgive me my transgressions
When I wish

When I pray
When I beg
To be reunited with you - soon, now, today
I know what this means
I know how this seems — ungrateful and obscene
That I would wish for my death when many would deem
My 'worldly possessions' a dream.
I would give all I have in a heartbeat if it meant I could find
myself with you
(All I own was not enough to 'save' you)
My darling Angel girl.

I gave birth to you
But you *made* me
You made me whole
You made me strong
You made me love more than I imagined possible
You were, you are, you forever will be
My inspiration, my guiding light
Oh, how you shine so, so bright!
I will never allow my dark, my pain, to dim your brilliant
luminescence
My darling Angel girl.

This world never deserved you
(Perhaps, neither did I)
And though I ache, and though I break

I will never let go of my gratitude
For the two thousand, three hundred and sixty-three days
you were with me.
The honour is real
The honour I feel to have been chosen as your parent
I will forever treasure this privilege
I will forever treasure your memory
My darling Angel girl.

You are where you need to be
Where you belong
Where you are whole
Where you are free.

My darling Angel girl
Please
Save a space for me.

~ ~ ~

Without You

There are so many people I love
So many that I care for
They love me too
I know they do

And yet, if I had the choice
Without a second thought
I would choose to be flying
Side by side
With only you.

My Angel girl...
It just doesn't make sense
To be living this life
Without you.

~ ~ ~

Angels Belong in Heaven

Some talk to me of religious faith
Telling me who I should worship
And laws I should live by.
They do not know
That faith alone keeps me alive
Faith that a reunion will take place
In a life after this.

Some tell me I should 'move on'
I shouldn't live in the past
I should keep myself busy.
They do not know
That even continuing to breathe
And getting out of bed each day
Is me moving forward
(Without you).

Some tell me you are by my side
Walking with me
Holding my hand through each day.
They do not know
That I do not want you to be here

For Angels belong in Heaven
And Heaven is where you must stay.

~ ~ ~

Dearest Darling Child of Mine

My love did not die with the passing on of your soul...

A big part of me vanished alongside your heartbeat
But my own heart remains - aching, bleeding
Encompassed within my weakening chest.

The blood in my veins did not freeze when yours did...

Nor did my soul manage to lock on to yours as you drifted
to the other side
It was chosen that I was to remain behind
Waving your pure light goodbye
Living within the four walls of memories
And photographs of your forever innocent smile.

My darling, I sometimes wonder
Who is brushing your hair and reading you bedtime stories
Forgive my jealousy
I cannot help but wish that it was me.

I miss you more than these words of mine can describe
And where the words run dry, I feel my soul begin to cry
But then, even the power of my pen is not enough to
prevent these tears from falling
Or stop me from calling out your name

As I live within this pain of your not being here
And my not being there.

Trapped in the truth of your never-ending absence
Dearest darling child of mine
All I can do is try to smile as I (impatiently) await the arrival
of my time
And imagine the beauty of your smiling face
As I wrap you in my arms
And you take me with you to the special place.

~ ~ ~

Come Back to Me

Things were different when you were here, my love
I knew who I was, I knew what I was doing
The pain I felt, the uncertain future, was justified.

I don't know now, I don't know anything
It's so scary, my love
I wish you were still here so that I could walk my path
knowing where I was stepping
You gave me strength, you gave me purpose, you gave me
me.

Is it selfish of me, my dear, to ask you to come back?
Is it crazy to think that there is a chance we can be
together again?
Why must I walk this earth without you?
Why must I make decisions I don't want to make, I'm
scared to make, I can't make?

Help me, my love
Come back to me and show me the way to go.

~ ~ ~

Your Smile

If I had to describe your smile
That smile, the memory of which outlived your little life
I would say it was *'golden'*
A blinding beauty that lit up the darkest of days, the
saddest of feelings
A smile that showed your inner beauty
That your non-existent voice was unable to explain.

Your pain and struggle would never diminish your desire to
share your light
My little star, you shone so bright
Always smiling through your fight
My purest, most incredible delight.

I lost you on a cold winter's night
But your smile lives with me every day.

~ ~ ~

Peace Lily

The way this peace lily in my lounge blooms so vibrantly, with its whites and greens
Often helps me to breathe a little easier
Like a sign that *you* are at peace.

The way it lets me know when it's thirsty and stands tall when I give it water
Makes me care for it even more
Like it's a part of me.
Like it's a part of *you*.

This peace lily, thriving beautifully in my lounge
Has been with me for 14 years.
That's 8 years more than you were
That's more than double the amount you lived.
It was gifted to me not long after you were born
And it's still going strong years after you've been gone.

The universe has allowed me the privilege to look after this peace lily
And though it would not have been my choice to care for it and not you, my girl
I understand. You had another place to be.

And though the ache in my heart is at times unbearable

At times suffocating
At times debilitating
I understand. You were too fragile for this world.
Too beautiful to remain.

I wonder sometimes how I will react when the day comes
that this peace lily will have to leave me, too...
It's strange to think that the demise of a plant will crush
my heart a little more than the mess it already is
But we humans attach things to memories, do we not?
We humans attach things to love.

Speaking of love...
I have never found a love that even comes close to that I
have for you, my one and only
For you, my only child.
That goes without saying, I know
And yet I need to say it
I need to tell you every day with the hope that you can
hear me.

I tell you as I kiss my cushion with a print of your beautiful
face on it
Every morning and every night
I tell you every time I see your star
And ache when it goes missing in the summer months
I tell you every time I visit your place of rest

I tell you as I live
I tell you as I breathe.

Memories and photographs are what I have now
To remind me of your beauty, of your grace
Memories and photographs of a little girl that will never
grow up
Never change, never smile again in her mother's embrace

Memories and photographs and this peace lily.

And I have faith
Faith that you are at peace
That you are now thriving, away from this world where
you were unable to thrive
That you are now walking, talking, running, dancing,
singing...
Heck, you are flying!
You are happy. You are FREE.

And so, I will wait for my time (impatiently) until I get to
see you again, my girl
I will wait, caring for this peace lily.

You see, to others this peace lily may be nothing but a
house plant

But to me... to me, it is love
To me, it is life
To me, it is a piece of *you*.

~ ~ ~

I Will Always Speak Your Name

I will speak your name...

I will speak of your life
And I will speak of your death.
I will speak of the joy you brought me
And I will speak of the pain I carry.

I will speak of my hope for our reunion when my time
comes
And I will speak of the days that I yearn for it to happen
'now'.

I will remind the world that you were here
And I will cry to the earth for life's order malfunctioning.

I will not hide my grief
Any more than I will hide my love
And I will not shy away from speaking of your short
existence.

I will never forget you
I will never let you be forgotten
And I will thank God every day
For having chosen me to be your parent.

I will speak your name
I will always speak your name...

KADER.

~ ~ ~

Unseeing

Fragmented eyes, measured blind
Gleaming through the wonders of your mind.
Sight distorted, unrecognised
Hidden in your soul, paralysed.

Triumphant moments, focused glare
A temporary smile with a beauteous stare
Feeling your identity pausing there.
An occurrence valuable, a happening rare.

~ ~ ~

*Kader was registered as blind but it was not known if the impairment
was with her vision or if it was her injured brain that didn't understand
what to do with her sight. I believe her eyes could see, as there were
times when she would look directly into my eyes. Those moments were
so beautiful.*

Night Sky

I scan the night sky looking for you
To shine your light into my glazing eyes
I long for the hope you carry for me, pour down on me
Instil in me
As I sit beneath your golden gleam
And dream of reunion.

Where are you, dear star?
Are you hiding from the world, as I am?
Has your light dimmed from the dark of your
surroundings?
Do you know that I love you?
Do you know that if I could breathe my life into you
My demise would be my greatest achievement?

Oh, dear star
The brightest, the most beautiful
So much I long to share with you
Come back to me, soon, won't you?
I am lonely here in your absence
And the sky looks bare without your luminescent smile.

Come back, please, come back!
I know it's not only me that's missing you
I know it's not only me

But I need you to return and be the light in my night sky
I need you to share the air that I breathe
I need to breathe!

I scan the night sky looking for you
Are you there, little star?
It's me, Mummy.

~ ~ ~

In the summer months, Betelgeuse is not visible in my part of the world. I feel so sad when I look up and I cannot see it.

A Mother's Grief [a Ghazal poem]

As if for you, all birds are singing grief
And all the church bells seem to ring in grief.

My heart does not accept the pain it holds
My cheeks grow raw from tears of stinging grief.

A child once here outlived by she who birthed
A story's ending ruined, bringing grief.

A mother's destined life without her child
No truer form of unforgiving grief.

There'll be no end for this, a longing ache
There is no human way of killing grief.

I must remain in absence of your form
A mourning mother - always living grief.

~ ~ ~

*'Her absence is like the sky,
spread over everything.'*

-CS Lewis

Section Three:
A Childless Mother

'...and now I'm here without you child,
what could be than this more tough?'

-SK Mustafa

Forced Improvise

No book was passed down
Through the ages
To teach us how to live life
After losing ones we birthed.

No teacher taught us
How to swallow overbearing emotions
After burying ones we carried
In our wombs
And in our arms
And in our hearts.

No life was predicted
In which we would use the earth
As a final blanket
To cover the owners of our second heartbeats.

No one explained
How to breathe
Through empty embraces
Or how to stay standing
When the weight of loss
Pushes down on our shoulders
Every day
Every minute.

We learn alone, bit by bit, day by day
We learn that there is no 'how'
There is only (forced) improvise.

~ ~ ~

Memories

All she has are photos now...
Photos of her biggest love, her only joy
Her greatest gift.
All she has are photos.

All she has are memories now...
Memories that make her smile, some that make her cry
Some that are slowly fading.
All she has are memories.

~ ~ ~

Pointless

What's the point in wondering what I could have done differently?
What's the point in carrying the guilt?
What's the point in imagining the teenager that she now would have been?
What's the point in aching for the pain that she lived in?

Where's the sense in making up scenarios in my head?
Of how my home would have felt with another heartbeat
Another set of lungs breathing
Another human with me, right now, in my arms
Forever my baby.

Where's the sense in crying that it was not meant to be temporary?

Who does it benefit to scream out the truth?
Where will it get me to roar out the words:
SHE IS DEAD
(and I am not)?

How will it help to wish with every ounce of my being
That it was the other way around?
Nothing will change.
Nothing will mend.

This is how it will be
Until my end.

An end that I long for
Every
Single
Day.

~ ~ ~

Because She Died

It's getting harder to know what to say
When people look at me and ask if I'm okay.
If I say yes, they see the lie
It's written all over my face.
When I say no, they ask me why
And it's always the same damned answer
'...because she died'.

~ ~ ~

Video Clips

I have chosen to stop watching
Video clips of babies crying when they're born.
Mine didn't
And when the deafening silence filled the room
It burned its way into my core.

> *The ashes reignite*
> *And the new born baby cries*
> *In those little video clips*

I have chosen to stop watching
Video clips of little girls that love to dress up just like mum.
Mine couldn't even speak the noun
Her brain would not allow it.

> *My eyes well up*
> *As the mum cries tears of joy*
> *In those little video clips.*

I have chosen to stop watching
Video clips of families gathered at a party for a child.
The memory of a gathering hits
A little girl's funeral
(And she hated big crowds, but that one would have made
her proud).

The cheering slices at my heart
And the child blows out the candles
In those little video clips.

~ ~ ~

Taken Too Soon

I howl to the Moon
In anger, in despair
'She was taken too soon!'
But the Moon can neither heal nor repair.

I pray to the Sun
To shine light on my pain
But the damage is done
There is nothing from prayer I can gain.

~ ~ ~

Dear Me

Dear... Me

I feel the pressure surround your eyes as you ready
yourself to cry
The tears, never-ending
There is no use in pretending
That your shattered heart is mending
It does not have to, does it?

In the absence of that divine (little) human
A shattered heart and eyes that cry without trigger
Are beyond
Expected
Accepted
Reflected (in the silence of her room)
Do not neglect it.

Let the salty oceans run free from your heavy eyes
Let your grieving be
Whether it be
Attacks by the tsunami of your intrepid tears
Or your smiles at your imagination's creativity and belief
Of angels dressed in pink and white, having parties of tea
Let your grieving be.

For how can a chest that carries a loss so immense
Cope with the tightness so tense
If not allowed to b r e a t h e ?

Dear... Me
Allow the suffocating silent screams to release

Dear... Me
Wrap your arms around her beautiful memory

Dear... Me
Without judgement or regret
Let your grieving be

It is a forever part of you
Dear Me

So let your grieving be free.

~ ~ ~

Makeup

There is no makeup strong enough
To hide the feelings from my face
So I leave my skin bare
And hope I just look tired

And I am tired
But more than that
I am hurting
But more than that
I am tired of hurting.

There is no makeup strong enough
To take the hurt away

And I am tired of sleeping
But it really is the only way.

~ ~ ~

Misunderstood

Will you listen?
Will you try to understand my unique reasoning?
I am different to you, yes
Different to him, to her
You see, God chose a life for me
Unlike the lives you're accustomed to see.

This age I have come to and still
It is difficult for me to accept
(But I do - what choice do I have?)
Still I love, still I care
As do some for me
Yet parts of my disposition cannot be typical
Cannot be changed (back).

This does not call for your judgement
Acceptance, yes, but the choice is yours
And your choice is fair
(I will not hold it against you).

You are free to decide
But so am I
To do what I can handle and leave what I cannot
To stay away from things, places, people that I cannot bear
(That I will not bear).

Respect my reasons, or don't
But do not take it upon yourself
To decide what I am
I know what I am
And this does not call for your judgement.

My grief does not belong to you
It is mine
And I am me
And this is the way I will always be.

~ ~ ~

Life Going On

Bass pounding from a song unrecognisable in the distance
Revving of cars across the road
Tick-tocking of a wall clock, tick-tocking of a desk clock
Sounds that would go unnoticed
If not for the quiet of this home.

A plane flying in the sky, so much louder than should be
Pedestrians passing by the window, heard with such clarity
The train behind the garden may as well be in the lounge
All proving there is life going on around this house
But not inside.

~ ~ ~

A Mother's Empty Embrace

Do you know what it means for a mother's embrace to be left empty?

If the birds were never to sing again
If the wind was never to blow
If the flowers were never to bloom again
It wouldn't matter. That's what it means.

Do you know what it means for a mother's embrace to be left empty?

If the sun was to stop shining
If the oceans were to dry out
If the world stops spinning
It wouldn't matter. That's what it means.
If tomorrow never comes
If today is the last day
If she stops breathing, now
It wouldn't matter. That's what it means.

This mother's embrace has been left empty
Her days full of longing, her smile bent out of shape
Her life upside down.

Do you know what it means for a mother's embrace to be left empty?

She is a mother without her child. That's what it means.

~ ~ ~

She Knows It Well

And between the instants when she is 'necessary'
She tries to block out the deafening silence
She tries not to dwell on the lack of an accompanying
heartbeat (or two, or three)
Or the missing figure in the background
She endeavours to direct her thoughts away from her
mapped-out solitude
The one she did not choose but has found herself trapped
within.

The miles of quiet habitat that surround her are cold
The sort of cold that inanimate heating cannot extinguish
or satisfy
She uses fleece blankets to warm her aching bones but her
heart is left bare
Or rather, full without destination.

Convincing herself that the sporadic moments of being
needed
Are enough to fill her wealth of time, she endures her
days, her years
And they pass, slowly yet fast
Silent, save for the internal screams that she muffles with
coffee and tobacco
Calls and texts

Naps and chocolate.

To some, the peace and quiet may sound a dream
But they do not know how sharp the stillness cuts when
inflicted
Without volition
Against free will
(She hopes they never will).

She knows it well enough for all.

Yes, she knows it
Well enough for all.

~ ~ ~

Nightmares

Not all nightmares are scary
Some break your heart. Some shatter your soul.

Like the ones where I have to ask permission from her
'owners' to hold her for a while
Like the ones where I have no place in her life
Like the ones where she begs me not to leave her
But I have to.

Like the ones that leave me howling and cold in the middle
of the night
Like the ones that take her breath away but not mine
Like the ones where she dies, then revives
Only to die again.

Trauma relived
Trauma revised
Trauma when I close my eyes.

Not all nightmares are scary
Some make you wish you had died.

~ ~ ~

I Will Love You

In my dreams I watch you sleep, like I used to
Listen to you breathe, like you used to
Feel the warmth of the life in your little body, where it
used to be
In my dreams, we are together.

In my prayers we will be together where you are now, in
paradise
Can you get me in?
Will you tell the Guard I miss you more than I wish to
Live?

In my head you exist, here, now
I speak to you - can you hear me?
In my head, only there, you talk back
With words I imagine, only in my head.

In my heart, my child, still a child
Are you still a child?
Or have you evolved into the unknown?
I do not know, I am not meant to know
But in my heart you are still my child.

And in me, in all of me, every ounce of me, there is you
Your essence, your memory

Your love, your beauty
Your existence.

In me, in all of me, there is you... there is you
And my God, my dear God, how I love you!

And forever, for my eternity
My child
I will love you.

~ ~ ~

My Reality

I never quite know when I wake up
If it was you there in my dream
It is just a feeling I am left with when I open my eyes
That I kissed your cheeks and kept you safe in my
everlasting embrace.

But I awaken to find my arms empty
And reality hits my longing heart.

Your light shines elsewhere, I know
Somewhere good
Somewhere deserving of your presence.

I will continue to search for that place in my dreams
And hope that one day my reality will be by your side.

~ ~ ~

With You

I only knew who 'me' was
As I held onto 'you'

For a short while
I felt worthwhile
Until destiny's raindrops
Poured down on us
And you were gone.

Now I'm here in this world
Without you
(My little you
My Angel you).

What is left for me?
Something (life) I cannot comprehend
Someone (me) I do not understand.

My tree of life has ended
No branches left
Just a lonely trunk
Not quite rooted into the ground
Of this Earth

And this Earth

Is not where I feel I should be.

I know I will only truly be 'me'
When I am once more with 'you'
(My little you
My Angel you).

~ ~ ~

What Am I Left With?

Memories merged with a thousand photos
Authenticity lessens somehow
I no longer have my child to hold
Tell me
What am I left with now?

Each day takes me further away
From our final warm embrace
When her delicate face my fingers did trace
Tell me
What am I left with now?

Am I being selfish feeling such pain
When I have no doubt she's in a better place?
How can I possibly help myself?
Tell me
What am I left with now?

~ ~ ~

Sunlit Words (of others)

Your sunlit words I cannot comprehend
Or maybe I just do not wish to understand
The rose coloured tint you paint upon my woe
It is not your pain - how the hell do you know?

You expect me to live life like I lived life before
But you cannot see behind my dead-bolted door.
Do you know what it's like to be in love with death
Because your hopes are gone and you remain devastated,
bereft?

I hope to God you don't, I pray you never do
Just accept I am different now and cannot be like you.
Certain things I've had to change, or choose to stay away
It is my choice to make - why are you being this way?

Allow me my pain, allow me my grief
Or you can choose to live in disbelief
That the old me is gone. This is me now.
I am proud how I cope, I don't even know how...

I get up every day, I continue to breathe
But some days I am crippled and struggle to believe
That I am meant to be here, without a clear purpose
So forgive me my friend, when I let my pain surface.

Just know I still care and I still want your company
But only you can decide if you want this current me
So here is the thing I am trying to say:
'Accept me as I am or turn your back and walk away.'

~ ~ ~

Justified

The heartache that I bear is justified my love
For I know you've found your peace in Heaven high above.

I'll carry out my days with you deep in my heart
Although life has been so hard since we have been apart.

Behind my jaded smile my eyes they shed some tears
But to know you're watching over me helps me overcome my fears.

This life it must go on, though you are far away
Until we meet again, when the time does comes one day.

Save a space for when I come and settle by your side
For the hope of this inspires me and fills my chest with pride.

We'll find ourselves together, united once again
So I promise to be strong and keep going until then.

~ ~ ~

The Truth

And the truth is
Though the years have mounted and passed
I still do not know how to do this
How to live without you
My one and only.

The truth is
With every smile at the beautiful children of others
I am reminded that you are not in my arms
With every photo that I look at of parents with their kids
I ache for the lack of mine
And I feel delight for them
As I burn for us.

The truth is
I struggle to accept my situation
The loving aunt, through blood or not, that has no living child of her own
The strong woman that has no choice but to be so
The lonely, grieving mother that lives together with a deafening silence
That could only be quashed with the voice of her child
But it is not
Nor will it ever be.

The truth is
That I am only holding on with the frail hope
That there will be an 'us' after this life of mine
And if I were to let go of this hope, I would have nothing
Not a thing to keep me here
Not a thing strong enough to aid my yearning, my aching
My indescribable grief.

The truth is
I will never quite know how to live without you
The truth is
I have no choice but to do so, every day.

~ ~ ~

Forevermore

Absence felt in the depths of a soul
A soul lost but held captive within a heart, broken
There is no escape from loss
No escape from yearning
No escape from a life, ever burning.

And there is not one but many
Many feel, many fear, many try to steer
Their lives forward through the dark clouds of blazing rainbows
And some succeed
And some fail
Some become stronger, and some frail.

Wondering are the minds
That are wandering through embargoes of self-love
Where did they go wrong?
Why are they not worthy?
Loss of desire may be the biggest loss of all
For if they desire not this life, what is left?

What is left when all hopes and prayers have been used up?
When the impossible is where one's hope is laid?

Answers are camouflaged too well to be found in life
Questions are but wasted thoughts of those living with pain
And so days go by, again and again.

Until that moment in a time unknown will come
It will appear
And souls and broken hearts and wondering minds
Will cascade into the surround where answers are found
And loss is no more

And pain will end, forevermore.

~ ~ ~

Acceptance Variation [a Villanelle poem]

Acceptance is not a constant
I have learned over the years
Some days acceptance lives, some days it does not.

It takes all that one has to attain their child has gone
And learn to live a life in their absence, but
Acceptance is not a constant.

The mind and body will fight to reject
The tragic loss, the unbearable pain
Some days acceptance lives, some days it does not.

When I look up at the sky with reception in my heart
I smile at the memory of my one and only, but
Acceptance is not a constant.

The calm surrounds when it is here
The storm sets in when it is not
Some days acceptance lives, some days it does not.

And though one grows around their loss
And grief is a little lighter when admitted
Acceptance is not a constant.
Some days acceptance lives, some days it does not.

~ ~ ~

I Lie

Can you hear it when I speak?
Can you feel the Hell in my voice?
I carry it within me, can you tell?
When I smile and look to have it in control
Do I make you trust that all is well?

Have I got you under my all deceiving spell?

You see, I lie
With each look at you I give
I lie
Each word a suffocating struggle
In disguise
I hide
Making myself look
Indestructible
All knowing
Ever glowing
Always growing.

In this journey of torment
I hide, I lie.

And you will not see through my veil (unless I let you)
It's too thick, it's too wide
The way it's supposed to be

(I'm not meant to speak my truth to you
Nor you your truth to me).

So I write the 'real' I do not speak
And offer up my feelings
Making myself look 'weak'
To you

But if I don't release the words in my heart
I will surely fall apart!

So today I'll write the truth
No more hiding and no lying
When you see me, looking 'normal'
More than likely, on the inside
I'm struggling, I'm screaming, I'm crying

But just know, and please believe
I am still, and always
Trying.

~ ~ ~

This Mask I Wear [a Rondeau poem]

This mask I wear to veil my face
Though hides the ache, cannot erase
A truth that I forever keep
That haunts me even as I sleep,
The hollowness her void creates.

So long has passed, my heart deflates
An emptiness meets my embrace.
My tears I fear will start to seep
This mask I wear.

I dream a fate that could replace
This life where cycle was misplaced
And as I think, I start to weep
My chest falls weak from hurt so steep.
No it will never quite encase,
This mask I wear.

~ ~ ~

'...and who said a mother's love can keep her child alive?'

-SK Mustafa

Section Four:
Milestones

'...and I'll celebrate alone
because you are not here'

-SK Mustafa

The Secrets of Winter

The secrets of winter whisper through the breeze
'Remember...'
Sending shivers through my soul.

Christmas's past and unwanted new years
Linger in my memory
And form shards of ice within my veins
Reminding me of pain
Reminding me of sorrow and broken tomorrows.

~ ~ ~

It's Your Birthday Again

It's your birthday again, there'll be so many more
And I'll celebrate alone because you are not here.

There's a smile on my face as I think of you today
But my teardrops fall because you are nowhere near.

I'll visit your grave but there will be no gifts
There will be no cards because you have gone away.

It's your birthday again - I will never forget it
A date engraved in my heart and there it will stay.

~ ~ ~

A Day I Dread Each Year

That day is coming, it's on its way
It will arrive as it always does
A day I dread each year.

How I wish I could change gear into reverse and hide away
I wish I could forever avoid this day.

A day for mothers
A day for children of any age to celebrate their mothers
But only those children that are still here.

Oh, how I wish I could change gear
And speed forward through the years
To the end... and then
I will dread this day no more
When the child I bore
Welcomes me into her world.

I will forget the pain of the past
When I hear the words I long for, at last
'Happy Mother's Day... Mum'.

$\sim \ \sim \ \sim$

Six Years – 28th January 2020

Six years ago today...

Six years since I lost a life in my embrace
Six years since I kissed her little face
And said 'let go now baby,
Don't worry about me'.

Six years and those years have been so long
Six years and still I feel I don't belong
In a world without her.

Six years and soon, so very near
She'll have been gone longer than she was even here
Six years and not a day goes by
That I don't feel to breakdown and cry
(and frankly, die)

Because what purpose has a mother
Without her (only) child?

Six years and the pain is overwhelming
Six years and I'm expected to now be okay
Six years and all I keep thinking
Is how many more years I have to live this way.

Six years too many, six years too much

Six years and I have had enough.

It doesn't get easier
It doesn't get less
This big rock of pain
I carry in my chest.

Six years...

And I will always remember
That night I kissed her
'Goodbye, forever'.
Six years ago today.

~ ~ ~

Friday 17th July 2020

This day, today, is marked and matched
It marks 2,363 days of Death
It matches the same amount of Life.

Any day after this, Death grows
As Life remains stuck in time
As Life remains stuck in time, forevermore.

This day, today, is marked and matched
Hereafter forever to be unmatched
As the days of Death outgrow those of Life
And so absence will beat down presence
And so absence will beat down presence, forevermore.

6 years, 5 months, 2 weeks and 4 days
The length of a little life that belonged to a little girl
The length of a little life that belonged to *my* little girl.

The length of a little life, lost within the days of mine -
My ever- growing
Ongoing
Never stopping life...
Unlike the life that did
Unlike the life that did

Unlike the little life that... *d i e d.*

2,363 days ago... she died
After 2,363 days of life.

And my days?
My days continue... continue... continue to grow.

And today it feels like 2,363 fucking lifetimes
And today it feels like... Death.

This day, today, is marked and matched.

~ ~ ~

Milestones [a Kyrielle sonnet]

'Tis hard to keep my tears at bay
I celebrate important days
Each year befalling, one by one.
Another milestone, passed and done.

Remembering your warm embrace
My eyes so long for your sweet face
My heart replaces you with none.
Another milestone, passed and done.

I never know how much the sting
Nor what distress the day will bring
If only I could hide or run.
Another milestone, passed and done.

I dread when days like this draw near
They shape, like fire covered fear
And there are times I come undone.
Another milestone, passed and done.

Still I will never not declare
Until I'm left without the air
That you were here, my shining Sun!
Another milestone, passed and done.

~ ~ ~

Tomorrow (Thirteen)

I don't want it to be tomorrow
Please don't allow tomorrow to be
Keep it away from me
Let me hide away from destiny.

I don't want to be able to say
'she *would* have been 13'
Nor ache for the fact that mum
to a teenager I *would* have been.

I don't want to have to lay
the flowers on her grave
I don't want to fill balloons
and send them up to Heaven.

I don't want it to be true that she never made it to 7.

I don't want to write these words
I don't want to cry these tears
I don't want to feel this pain
I don't want to count the years.

The years that have to pass
Before I can kiss her face
The years that have to pass

For her to be in my embrace.

I don't want to live this life another day without her here.

I don't want it to be tomorrow
I don't want it to be today
I don't want it to be a day
I want it all to go away.

I don't want it to be tomorrow.

~ ~ ~

Christmas Time

Dreaded days of December
Followed by another January of yet another New Year
I wish I could hide
I wish I could make these months disappear
I wish I could sink into a time with no surrounding cheer.

Family photos and celebrations
Gifts and happy children
Excited children
Other people's children
Living children

And me.

I wish I could make myself disappear.

~ ~ ~

The Night Before Christmas (2013)

A Christmas Eve unlike any other
A little girl stops breathing, briefly
In the arms of her screaming mother.

There is no other soul around
For just the two of them
This awful moment was bound.

And as her mother reaches for the phone
The little girl starts to breathe

And as her mother cries with relief
The little girl now sound asleep.

~ ~ ~

A Frozen Moment

Just like that, in one frozen moment
The warmth of your embrace was taken from me.
I would forever be lost in a daydream that plays like a
nightmare on a loop.
My wistful winter wishes were doomed to remain pleading
for reunion.
The price of love, a mother's love
Became chains of grief strangling my soul.

A frozen moment
Relived each year.

~ ~ ~

'Each year befalling, one by one,
another milestone, passed and done.'

-SK Mustafa

Section Five:
Grief's Battle

'...and just like that,
without a trigger,
grief's darkness says hello.'

-SK Mustafa

Grief Attacks

I feel you, creeping
Readying yourself to attack
And take possession
I have memorised the sound of your footsteps.

No longer will I beg you to leave me alone
I am ready
I am not ready
It doesn't even matter anymore.

I'll see you soon.

~ ~ ~

Explosions of Grief

Tiny sparks in the shape of random reminders
Of how it was
How it should have been. The things that could have been.

Tiny embers of memories not made
Memories tainted by broken dreams and damaged lives.
Memories stolen by death.

Tiny flames fanned suddenly, quickly, forcefully
By triggers so easily obtained
Hiding behind any moment.

Tiny fiery particles blowing up in a mind that yearns
hibernation
A heart in foetal position
A human longing for an end.

Tiny glowing bodies of ignited tears, to start with
Until the blazes begin to roar like almighty lions at war
And explosions of grief erupt.

~ ~ ~

I Forget Sometimes

I forget sometimes
How to breathe
For a split second, for an instance
When all I hear, my child
Are the silent cries
Of your post-existence.

~ ~ ~

Trapped (Grief's Anxiety)

I don't want it anymore!

I don't want to be a bereaved mother
I don't want to have to miss my girl with no way of getting to her
I don't want to look at other people's children and feel anger, then guilt
I don't want to keep wondering what she would have been like had she lived
Had she not been brain damaged, disabled, ill.
I don't want it!

I don't want it!
But there is no alternative
Not one
I'm trapped. For life.
There is no other side of this
There is no getting over this
There is no escape from this
I'm trapped. For life.

I, one who fears not being in control
I have been placed in the ultimate trap
A position where no control is possible.
I don't want it anymore!

Who do I turn to?
Where can I run to?
Who can take this away?
Who can make it not be?
No one! Nowhere!

It is a huge weight engraved within my soul
Too heavy to be removed
Too solid to be broken
It's stuck there, it's trapped.

I'm trapped.
I don't want it anymore!

~ ~ ~

Grief's Battle

Wishing each day away into a nightmare
I trudge through the trenches of never-ending grief
Laying my haggard body uncaringly atop
The explosives rigged inside my shattered heart.

I walk alone in this war encompassed by my soul
Wishing upon no person to fight by my side
Or even as my enemy, for I could never be
Cruel enough - this combat is far too rough.

Carrying battle gear upon my breaking back
I fight this conflict on my own
Dodging through the bullets of my destined path
Never knowing what awaits me at its end.

Yes, eventually it will fall to its end
Confrontation with my reality will be over
And maybe there on that concluding day
Finally, this grief will be blown away.

~ ~ ~

Make It Through

Outside the sun is glaring
Inside the storm is brewing
Closing in from the East, South, North and West
There is nowhere I can escape to.

At best, I can hope it passes soon.
At best, I can pray I make it through.

~ ~ ~

The Two Sides of My Grief

She is in eternal peace.
The struggle and pain she faced in human form is no longer.
She is flying high, pirouetting like a fairy across the sky,
Thriving within the realms of paradise.
She is free. She is where she is supposed to be.

I am left behind, childless. Alone.
My embrace aches for the only being I grew within my womb.
My eyes scan my surroundings for the smiles she would grace me with through her discomfort.
I fight to understand my continued existence.
I am growing weak under the heaviness of my grief.
I am breaking.

Her short existence will never be forgotten.
The effect of her life continues to ripple with the smiles of others
Of those that met her, of those that did not.
She met her purpose and left behind a beauty of a different kind.
Her life was not in vain. She is loved. She IS love.

I am struggling to stand.

My shattered heart is tearing me apart.
I scream to be taken, to be reunited.
My tears drown my forced smile into the darkness of
my pain.
I am cold. I am burning. I am oh so very tired.

The two sides of my grief, living together.
Loving and tormenting each other.
I am a Mother
Yet all I have to prove it is a scar across my abdomen
And the photographs hanging on my wall.

~ ~ ~

Enough! [a double Tanka poem]

'Tis oh so vicious!
Brewing constantly beneath
A burning wave, still
'Til walls crumble under weight
And angst attacks the smashed heart.

'Tis oh so severe!
When times of harsh grief ascend
Following the calm
And one lays upon the floor
And cries, beseeching *'ENOUGH!'*.

~ ~ ~

Silence

The dictionary does not define silence in the way it harvests a soul
You yearn for quiet
But peace is not connected to noise
Any more than company is the answer to loneliness.

Reasoning often quells the questions asked by shallow minds
Yet, 'why?' is not ours to ask.

And who said breathing comes naturally?
And who said a mother's love can keep her child alive?

Lies are for the weak-minded
But hearing truth is a blind man's game.

And neither do I want to hear nor do I want to see
And neither do I wish to speak nor do I choose to be

Yet here I am
Reborn with every rising of the sun
Going to sleep, only to wake up again and again.

Some children die
Some are left alone

And a mother is left empty handed, placed in the cold
Poisoned by the fumes of cigarettes and empty bedrooms.

And their paths will never cross
The silence will remain

And I go to sleep, only to wake up again and again.

~ ~ ~

She is Gone

And when the waves of grief come crashing
Everything turns
        d a r k

The pain
Burns like acid coursing through my veins
And a few tears are not enough
       To breathe I must howl.

To breathe is not my choice
       Neither living
       Neither being.

She is gone
I am not

And everything is
       d a r k.

~ ~ ~

Darkness Takes Over

Darkness takes over
As she considers that there may be no life after this
A thought that paralyses her being
For you see, this would mean only one thing
That she would not be reunited with her child, her only love.

How can she accept that the longing in her heart, the devastating pain
Will not be compensated in an afterlife?
Memories of cupping a beautiful little face in her hands
Holding a tiny hand in hers
Taking in the smell of her child's scent
Looking into the eyes of an extension of herself
Memories of her daughter's touch
Memories that have not destroyed her
For the belief of a time after this
Where they will be together again.

But darkness takes over
As she considers that there may be no such time
No such place, no such life
Oh, the destruction within her mind
Within her body
As the thought of such a possibility settles.

She wonders
If those that tell her to move on, to find happiness
Can fathom the reality
Of waking up each day with this deep rooted, never-
ending
Devastation
The sound of a mother's inner voice
Screaming, screaming, screaming
'I miss my child'
'I want my child'
'I need my child'.

A reality she would wish upon no one
Yet, a reality that she lives every day
Every moment
With the hope, the desperate hope
Of a meeting that will take place at the end
A hope that allows her to breathe in the absence of her
girl.

Except when darkness takes over
As she considers that there may be no such ending.

~ ~ ~

Grief Will Underlie

Forever grief will underlie
Behind each joyful laugh
Each bright-eyed smile
Loss will always loom.

A void in a home
Marked by silence
A room painted pink
In memory instead of in use.

Certain things in life
Unchanged by time
Certain things final
Like their last goodbye.

Like a last kiss planted
On a paling face
The final prayer whispered
Followed by *'let go now, child'*.

Still, tomorrows keep on coming
The clouds keep on floating
And a sun is born each day
Wanted or unwanted, it is so.

But forever grief will underlie
And it will be so until a calling comes
When it is time for time to end.

Condemned to Grieve

The Devil rages his storm within me
Standing back and watching, gleefully
As he disregards my piercing screams and pleas
For mercy. *'Mercy!'*
But he is not done watching my suffering.

My wailing cries are like music to his fire
And I burn in his flames
I burn in torment, in agony
In His never ending blaze of torturous glee.

He watches me writhe and fight His affliction
And laughs at my failure to accept His control
And he loves to dance to the tune of my pain
And dance he does
As I battle and lose
Again and again.

It never ends. It will never end.
This is my story
I am condemned.

~ ~ ~

Not All Scars Heal

Not all scars do heal
Some are only held together by flimsy strands of silk
That often snap, then reform
And snap, then reform

And every memory of every prior injury
And every blow from every new injury
Does strike at that old scar and peel the wound wide open

And it bleeds... oh, how it bleeds!

Years pass but still
No new pain, however small, can be carried unrelated
To the ultimate
To the substantial
Always ripping to shreds the weak stitching that holds
together that one, unhealable scar

And it bleeds... oh, how it bleeds!

And those not affected will never understand
And those not affected will think that she seeks sympathy
For they will wonder how it can be
That all that she lived before
And all that she has lived since

And all that she will continue to live
Be related, always, to that one
That one, painful impairment

They cannot fathom
That not all scars do heal
And that before them stands a matriarch without her tribe
For the universe chose to split them apart
And as the tribe flies free in the heavens
The one left behind carries the incurable scar
And when the breeze hits a little too hard
Or the sun shines a little too hot
And when the burdens come in the masses
Or affliction climbs on board

She bleeds! She bleeds! She bleeds!
Oh, how she bleeds!

Yet she holds her position, weak or strong, in the pool of
her own blood
She fights to keep infection out of her cavernous lesion
And her screams are sometimes heard by all
Sometimes none at all
And heavy she does fall
But each and every time she stands back up, tall

Even as she bleeds

And oh, how she bleeds!

There have been many before her
And more will come hereafter
And they will learn
While the unaffected never will
That not all scars do heal.

~ ~ ~

It Hits

It hits, you know
A sudden wave of devastation
Not out of the blue
Just out of sync with the current mood
But who said grief is disciplined?
There is no barrier for the pain
Of a broken hearted mother.

It hits
Sometimes cripples
Sometimes chokes
Not that it ever disappears, you understand
Just, at times, the waves are calmer
And the thought of paradise is soothing.

But then, sometimes, when it hits
It just feels too hard to breathe.

~ ~ ~

Combat

I am armed once again with my ancestral kilij
Waving it from left to right
Fighting off the thoughts that try to invade my weakening
mind.
I try to keep my solitude and grief in the light
But while the sun singes my aging flesh
My mind is battling the Dark Knights.

Distraction has eluded me.
Solitude gives way to battles destined to be lost
And my sword weighs heavy in my hold.

Behold!
Here they march forth
One dark, two dark - too damned dark to fight with light.
Yet I fight, each and every day
And the blood of my child runs heavy through my veins.

It is all in vain, I know it
But my heart, my grieving heart, can no longer remain
stoic
And my mind is so damned far from heroic.

I fight to protect them
Though what have I to gain any longer?

The title of 'Mother' has escaped me
And the name of 'Woman' seems to hate me.
I am a daughter, a sister, an aunt, a friend
Yet none hold the strength of 'Materfamilias'
(The female head of a household).

I am not that.
I am no longer that.

My home as bare as a dead man's stare.
My embrace has no offspring to bear, despite having birthed one
Now buried and gone.
Where is my capacity to care if I live or die?
Disappeared with the fading of her innocent eyes.

Yet I fight!
I still fight!
I must fight!
For the burden of those who care is yet another weight I carry.

Exhaustion is not an option.
'God give me strength! God give me strength!'
I cry as I march into combat.

My demise must not be that of my own war.

That does not suit the creature that my mother bore
Nor the bearer of my own child.

I will defeat!
No matter how bruised and bloody my metaphorical feet
As I march and feud through the valley of my dark.

Weapons clash, clang and spark!
Light is beating down the Dark!
Hark! One more battle I have won.
Over and out and done.

I will see you again, my friend
I will see you again in the next one.

~ ~ ~

Wreckage

When I look at too many photos of my girl
Of us, with her in my arms
Where she was not destined to remain
Where she smiled and thrived to love me through her pain
The reality that I will never get to hold her again
Rushes in and turns warmth into ice cold running through my veins
And there is no real way to explain...
The devastation.

When I spend too much time reminiscing, thinking
Of us together, a mother with her only child
My breathing feels... deterred
Life becomes unbearable in a murky blur
My words begin to stagger and slur
As I ask *'why not me instead of her?!'*
And the attack of grief, like demons in the shadows, begins to stir...
The devastation.

It is a heavy load to carry
A heart torn to shreds weighs down on a soul with unmeasurable force
And living can feel like slow death
As the anguish and the sorrow

And the torture of another (childless) tomorrow
Haunts and suffocates and radiates....
The devastation.

And there is no real way to summarise
The grief of my situation
And there is no real way to describe
My devastation.

~ ~ ~

'...and when the pain hits too hard,
sleep is her only safeguard.'

-SK Mustafa

Section Six:
A Grieving Mother's Faith

'When you are sorrowful, look again in your heart and you shall see that in truth you are weeping for that which has been your delight.'

-Gibran Khalil Gibran

What I Imagine

Dancing with angels, singing and laughing
In blue crystal seas with dolphins you're swimming
Flying through clouds so pink and so fluffy
That's what I imagine, that's what I see.

Feelings of happiness and pure delight
Tea parties with fairies all dressed in white
A smile on your face so wide and so bright
That's what I imagine, that's what I see.

Gardens and forests through a magical door
Animals and wildlife you've not seen before
So much to learn and see and explore
That's what I imagine, that's what I see.

Memories you gather to share and explain
Excited yet patient, you're waiting for me
Saving my space and keeping it warm
That's what I imagine, that's what I see.

~ ~ ~

With Endings Come New Beginnings

Halos formed through dust and breeze orbit the innocent
Sunflowers wilt with final breaths as lives are released into
open skies
Tears of those left behind seep nourishment deep within
Earth's core.

Heaven's gate shines bright as new souls are welcomed
into golden fields.

Endings breathe life into beginnings.

Your Message

A dream it was, though it felt so real
In your earthly state, I was feeding you.
You, smiling so brightly, taking your sweet time.

Our mouths did not move, but we communicated.

'Come on, baby girl. You have to eat to build up your strength. To grow.'
'Don't worry, Mummy, I am eating. I am never left hungry. I am full and I am well. Please let Nanny and Grandad know too.'

A smile dawned on my face as I awoke.
You had given me your message.

Thank you, my Angel.

~ ~ ~

A Sign on Your Birthday

A beautifully still night it was
The sky was clear
The stars were gleaming.

Your birthday
Spent with family
Celebrated in your absence

And as the date was near to change
One stranded balloon I found
One that had gotten away
Hiding in the corner of my kitchen
Pushing at the ceiling.

I took it into the night
And let it go
To find its way to you.
White and bright
It was clear in the darkness as it flew
Until it disappeared
And just as it did, a shooting star
Shot across the sky
I couldn't believe my eyes!

What a wonder!
What a delight!

A sign from you
A beautiful message in the night.

A Dream

A dream full of you
The feeling of you in my arms
Your delightful expression as you held me so tightly.

A dream full of you
One I wish could play on repeat
With me watching over you instead of the other way around.

A dream full of you
And how I have missed you
Since the angels took you to play.

A dream full of you
My beautiful, perfect you
A dream I wish would come true.

~ ~ ~

Scenarios

I wonder about these scenarios in my head
Ones that are not in line with my life
Are they glimpses of a parallel universe?

Some so full of joy
Fragments of a life I long for
Could they be reality in another realm?
A life ongoing, starring another me
Where my losses never happened
And my heart remains intact?

You see, these scenarios in my head
Are all that keep me company some days
I forget
I let go
I get lost in them
And for a while the pain ceases to exist.

And yes, some days they drive me crazy
When I spend too much time wondering
'Could these events be real?'
When I let myself crave for a life that includes
Such comforts
Such joy
Such beauty.

These scenarios in my head
Maybe they cause more harm than good
Some days.

Still, I will not let go of them
You see, in a way they give me hope
A slice of comfort almost
That *this* is not all there is
That *this* is not all there will be
That the experiences I have lived are but a small part
Of an overall existence
That there is more, so very much more
Than *this*.

And while the hope and comfort continues
As a result of these scenarios in my head
They will remain my loyal friends
And I will keep them with me always.

~ ~ ~

Maybe

Maybe...
As one soul leaves this world
Another one enters
Encountering one another along the way.

Sharing thoughts while crossing paths
Connected in ways known only to them
In that moment of transition.

Love dies momentarily
To be reborn in a new set of eyes.

Maybe...
I am connected to you
And you to me.

Maybe, just maybe...
We were meant to be one
One form. One love. One phenomenon.

Maybe.

~ ~ ~

Waiting

A sense of missing
Nostalgia. Reminiscing.
A bare embrace
Absence of a beautiful face.

Years of rising sun
With you where you begun.
Tears of crimson grief
Existence based belief.

Awaited ending
Reunion pending.

~ ~ ~

Jealousy vs Gratitude

Who brushes your hair now, baby girl?
Who sings you lullabies to help you sleep?
Who holds you when you're crying?
I so wish it was still me.

I am jealous, I admit it
And yet my gratitude is endless
For whoever it is that cares for you
The way that your mother used to.

~ ~ ~

Sweet Child of My Descent [an Elegy]

Oh, sweet child of my descent
How I loved thee, Heaven sent
How I love thee still, though away you be
Thy mem'ry resides forever within me.

Photographs surround me always
Filling my eyes with beauty each day
I gaze at thy innocent face
And wonder of your happy place.

My heart doth ache for your delightful form
And for your presence I forever mourn
But there will come a time, of this I'm confident
When a union with you will end my grieving torment.

Oh, sweet child of my longing womb
As I sit here, thinking of you, in this lonely room
Know that I smile at thought of an end
Where mother and child will unite, once again.

~ ~ ~

We Will Meet Again

No more struggle
No more pain
It's time to return from where you came.

Thank you for your presence
Thank you for your strength
Thank you for each and every single breath.

Farewell, sweet one
Goodbye, my love
Let the angels guide you to the above.

It's time, dear child
To take your leave
We *will* meet again – I believe.

~ ~ ~

*'...I'll try to make my way to you
in Heaven up above.'*

-SK Mustafa

Additions

My Truth [a Spoken Word poem]

I'd like to speak to you for a while
But I know that what I have to say may make some of you
want to walk away
And that's okay.

You see, I have a child... who died
My only child who was here for just a while
6 years and 5 months to be precise
And she, my goodness
The apple of my eye!
My only sunshine.

She was ill and damaged
And was often in pain, but she managed
To smile a smile that would light up the room
With such grace
She had the most beautiful little face!
Sure I may be biased
But which mother isn't?
And which mother doesn't want to talk about her child?
You see, that doesn't change if that child has sadly died.

Sometimes when I think of her I breakdown and cry
But every time that I think of her, I smile
Grief has a way to teach a person

That you can carry your pain every minute of every single day
But smile, and love and live through it anyway.

Are you still listening?
Are you wondering why I would choose to talk about the unimaginable?
Well, I can imagine it, I'm living it.
And I will not lie
Nor will I EVER deny, that my
Little girl was here and she survived longer
Than they ever thought she would
And she made me so fucking proud!
Why would I not want to shout out loud:
'My child existed! She was here!'

And when I talk of her don't try to change the subject
Because you're afraid that I'll cry when I remember her
Do you think that I forget about her for even a second?

But here's the thing...
My normality had to change
My truth can be hard for others to bare
To listen to, to discuss, to consider
And I get it, I do, but I ask this of you
May God and the heavens forbid, if you were in my shoes

Wouldn't you want the basic human right of speaking your truth?

I own it
My life, my grief
My truth that of course I wish I was with my girl
And you and I both know what that means
But what is more natural than a mother wanting to be with her child?!

I know, I know I have to survive
Whether the reason is obvious every day or not
I am here and until my time comes, here I'll remain
And I will continue to speak of my little girl
And I will continue to speak her name –
Kader. Kader. Kader.
It means Destiny. She lived her destiny, and I am living mine.

So... I just wanted to speak to you for a little while
And share the biggest piece of my life.
But I know that what I had to say has made some people walk away and that's okay
I will continue to speak my truth anyway.

~ ~ ~

Loss of a Child – The Forbidden Subject!
[an unpublished 'article' from 13 July 2017]

It has been three and half years since my daughter passed away. She was 6 years old. In the years following her death, on top of the (obvious) pain I have been living with, I have also come to realise that the subject of my child – be it her life or her death – is a very taboo subject indeed. With people who knew her, or those who didn't, reactions are almost always awkward and uncomfortable. Understandably so. Of course this topic is an extremely sad one. Unimaginable. Who can bear to think of how painful it must be to outlive their child? Even the idea of it is heart-breaking. Fact. However, in an age where awareness is being sought for so many different things, where topics that were once almost forbidden are now being discussed openly, I can't help but feel that it is time that bereaved parents should also have a voice.

Now, I am fully aware that I am only one person and I have no right or power to speak on behalf of all bereaved parents. What I am discussing here are my own personal thoughts and feelings. So, here I go...

My child was here. She did exist. She had a name, a face, a personality. She was, and still is, my daughter and I was, and still am, her mum. I know you get that – it goes without saying. But do you understand that I need her to not only be remembered but to be talked about, freely without 'fear'. Say my daughter's name – KADER. Ask me about her. What she liked; what she disliked; how she reacted to things. Okay, so in my case, my girl was extremely disabled and so there were a lot of things she couldn't do or understand. You can ask me about that, too. I want it known, remembered and never forgotten that I am a mum. A proud one. The way you discuss your child, I want to discuss mine.

As I said earlier, I can't nor am I trying to be anyone else's 'voice'. However, I have read comments and posts by so many other bereaved parents that read 'say my child's name'. Yes, we want our kids to be remembered and to continue existing even though they are no longer physically with us. I don't statistically know how many of us there are in the world. What I do know is that there are a LOT of us. Mums and dads that have buried their child(ren). Whether our child(ren) died in an accident, whether they were murdered, whether they died suddenly or after years of illness; some were babies, some were teenagers, some were adults - we all have one thing in common – we belong to a 'club' that no one would ever choose to become a member of. We are labelled. We are 'bereaved parents'. Yet, we are parents nonetheless and we are here – talk to us! Ask us questions about our kids' lives and even their deaths. Will it bring tears to our eyes? Quite possibly. Will it remind us and break our hearts? Of course not! There isn't a second that goes by where we forget that our child has died. Our hearts will never be unbroken. The knowledge, the pain, the fact is with us every second of every day – whether we are locked away crying our eyes out; at the cinema with our friends; on a date night with our partners; even when we are laughing and having fun... we know. It's there, always.

Of course, there are those of us who don't want to talk about it. There are many different types of people, full stop. Some like to talk about things – problems, events, personal lives – and some don't. I can tell you that I have always been one to talk about things openly, as I am sure you have figured out by now! I also know that if someone doesn't want to discuss something, whatever it is, they will just say so. It is not any different when the subject is our lost children. Fair enough?

So please, say her name; say his name; say their names. Tell us something you remember. Ask us what you have forgotten. Discuss the things you want to know about our children but may have felt before now would be too upsetting for us to talk about.

On my behalf, I promise I will always welcome the subject of my daughter with gratitude and a smile.

~ ~ ~

About the Author

SK Mustafa

My name is Sonay (*pronounced 'sonn eye'*) Mustafa but I go by SK. I am second generation Turkish Cypriot, born and raised in London, UK. The 'K' in my penname 'SK Mustafa' is my daughter, Kader's, initial.

I started writing in 2014, shortly after Kader passed away and I haven't stopped since. Initially, I wrote poems solely about my grief, but over the years I have expanded the genres of poetry that I write. I also dabble in short stories now and then. Writing has been my saviour and I couldn't be without it now.

I always knew I would compile my grief poetry into a book one day. It took me seven years to get to the point where I felt ready. I do hope that you found this book worth reading.

Thank you.

Sincerely yours,

www.skmustafa.co.uk
Instagram: @s_k_mustafa

Made in United States
Orlando, FL
22 October 2024

53000915R00091